Native Americans

The Apache

Richard M. Gaines

ABDO Publishing Company

visit us at
www.abdopub.com

Published by ABDO Publishing Company, 4940 Viking Drive, Suite 622, Edina, Minnesota 55435. Copyright © 2000 Abdo Consulting Group, Inc., Pentagon Tower, P.O. Box 36036, Minneapolis, Minnesota 55435 USA. International copyrights reserved in all countries. No part of this book may be reproduced in any form without written permission from the publisher.

Published 2000
Printed in the United States of America.
Second printing 2002

Illustrators: Kevin Shives (pgs. 7, 19, 23); David Kanietakeron Fadden (pg. 11)
Interior Photos: Jane Winiecki (page 15)
           Corbis (pgs. 9, 13, 17, 18, 21, 25, 27)
Editors: Bob Italia, Tamara L. Britton, Kate A. Furlong
Art Direction & Maps: Pat Laurel
Border Design: Carey Molter/MacLean & Tuminelly (Mpls.)

Library of Congress Cataloging-in-Publication Data

Gaines, Richard M., 1942-
    The Apache / Richard M. Gaines.
      p. cm. -- (Native Americans)
    Includes bibliographical references and index.
    Summary: Presents a brief introduction to the Apache Indians including information on their society, homes, food, clothing, crafts, and life today.
    ISBN 1-57765-381-5
    1. Apache Indians--Juvenile literature. [1. Apache Indians. 2. Indians of North America--New Mexico.] I. Title.

E99.A6 G25 2000
979'.004972--dc21

                                      99-059867

Contributing Editor: Chris Coder

Chris Coder has a Masters degree in anthropology from Northern Arizona University. He has been an archaeologist on the Colorado Plateau and high plains since 1980. He currently works as a consultant to the Yavapai-Apache Nation. Chris lives with his family near Flagstaff, Arizona.

Illustrator: Kevin Shives

Kevin Shives is a tribal member and graphic artist of the Yavapai-Apache Nation in Camp Verde, Arizona. Currently, he is attending college full-time to obtain a degree in 3D computer animation.

Contents

Where They Lived 4

Society 6

Homes 8

Food 10

Clothing 12

Crafts 14

Family 16

Children 18

Myths 20

War 22

Contact with Europeans 24

Geronimo 26

The Apache Today 28

Glossary 31

Web Sites 31

Index 32

Where They Lived

The Apache and the Navajo moved from northern Canada to their new desert homeland around A.D. 1200. The Apache settled in the deserts, plains, and mountains of the Southwest.

The Apache were divided among many extended families and clans. One of the larger groups was the Jicarilla Apache. They lived in northeastern New Mexico.

The Mescalero Apache lived western Texas and southeastern New Mexico. The Mimbreños lived in southwestern New Mexico. The Chiricahua Apache lived in southern Arizona and northern Mexico. The Dilzhee (Tonto), Aravaipa, and Coyotero lived in central and eastern Arizona. The Lipan lived in Kansas.

Desert lands of the Southwest

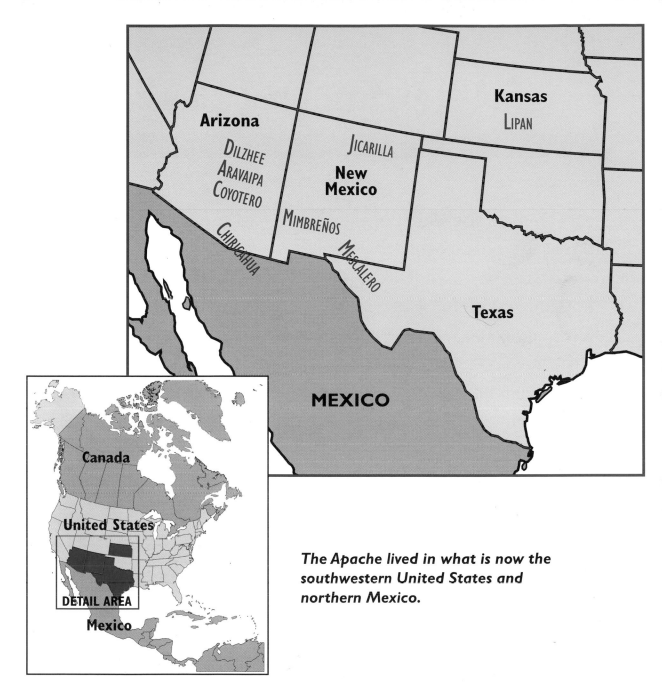

The Apache lived in what is now the southwestern United States and northern Mexico.

Society

The main social unit of the Apache was the family group. Most camps had two to five families.

Each camp had a leader, usually the husband of the oldest mother. The leader was responsible for the group's well being. By example, the leader reminded everyone of their duty to the family and their clans' **traditions**.

When a girl came of age, she went through a Sunrise Ceremony. When it was over, she was considered a woman of the tribe.

When a son married, he moved to his wife's mother's camp. The son remained an **ally** of his parents' camp. In times of trouble or war, a family called on their son and his family for help. This way, the Apache created strong **bonds** among groups who lived far apart.

A young Apache woman stands inside a *gowa'a* during a Sunrise Ceremony. Each of the four poles faces one of the four sacred directions. Each is decorated with symbols. Eagle feathers are strung above the East entrance.

The Apache Sunrise Ceremony, or *na'ii'ees,* is a four-day ceremony. Apache girls experience it when they become women of the Apache Nation. For four days and nights, the girls dance to songs and prayers. They participate in sacred rituals. The girls also receive and give gifts and blessings.

Homes

An Apache family lived in a grass and brush home called a *wickiup*. To build a *wickiup*, the Apache set four juniper **saplings** in the ground. Then, the saplings were tied together to make a sturdy frame.

Next, tamarisk, cottonwood, oak, sumac, or willow saplings were spaced around the base of the circle. These were then bent in an **arc** and tied to the other saplings for support.

Yucca leaves and other desert plants were collected for the roof. In wetter areas, bear grass was used. It was picked with the roots attached. This way, it stayed fresh longer.

To make the roof, yucca leaf **fibers** were made into cord. The roof material was stitched around in bundles from the bottom up. A small hole was left in the top of the *wickiup* to let smoke out. The outer base was banked with dirt. The doorway always faced east to greet the morning sun. It was covered with a hide or blanket.

An Apache family in front of their wickiup (1878)

Food

There was little rain each year in the Southwest. But, the Apache were experts at surviving on the desert's few **resources**. Apache women collected acorns, seeds, cactus fruit, and other plants for food and medicine.

The Apache hunted buffalo, antelope, and deer. When these animals could not be found, the Apache lived on rabbits and other small game. The Apache did not eat bears, turkeys, fish, or snakes.

When the Spanish came to America, they moved onto Apache lands. In **retaliation**, the Apache raided their settlements for cattle and other food.

Some Apache had gardens of corn, melons, and pumpkins. They also made a drink from corn called *tulapai*. *Tulapai* was made for special occasions.

An Apache woman tends corn

Clothing

The Apache wore **tanned**, deerskin clothes. Usually, the clothes were decorated with long **fringes**. The clothes were also painted with single-color designs.

The women wore wraparound skirts. They also wore simple **ponchos** as shirts. The men wore **breechcloths**, buckskin leggings, and shirts decorated with beads. And they carried blankets and Mexican **serapes**. Both men and women wore deerskin shawls.

Apaches were famous for their knee-high buckskin boots. The boots were often decorated with fringe or silver **conchos**. They traded these boots with their neighbors for things like salt, blankets, and guns.

After the Europeans arrived, the Apache wore cotton shirts and skirts. Apache women even wore **petticoats** beneath their skirts.

An Apache woman in traditional dress

Crafts

Apache women carried all of their families' possessions in baskets. These baskets were woven from the shoots of desert shrubs and young trees. A basket that carried water was called a *tus*.

A *tus* was made from lemmonberry and cottonwood shoots. In the spring, these shoots were cut in four-foot (1.2 m) sections. These sections were cut lengthwise into three pieces. Then, they were woven together to make the bottom of the *tus*.

The woven pieces were **coiled** to form the outside shape of the *tus*. The coils were sewn tightly together with yucca plant strips.

To make the baskets watertight, they were brushed with melted piñon tree sap. The sap hardened just like a **varnish**, and sealed the *tus*.

Woven baskets and bowls

Earthen pot with wooden cooking utensils

Shallow basketry bowl

Family

Parents usually arranged marriages. The groom's parents offered gifts to the bride's family. If the bride's family accepted the gifts, the couple was considered married.

The groom moved to the bride's mother's family camp. He brought food for everyone to share. But he was forbidden to ever speak to his mother-in-law. Eye contact between them was considered bad manners.

Children were always welcome in an Apache home. European children captured in **raids** and **orphaned** Native Americans were raised as sons and daughters. Apache children were trained from an early age to be mentally tough and physically **disciplined**.

When girls were five or six, mothers and grandmothers taught them basket weaving and other crafts. When boys were five or six, fathers and uncles took them into the desert and mountains. There, the boys learned how to hunt and fight enemies in the Apache way.

An Apache chief and his family

Children

Apache babies were carried on their mothers' backs while bundled on a **cradleboard**. The cradleboard was often hung in a tree around the home. This way, the baby could watch the family's daily activities. When the baby was old enough to walk, he or she helped the mother gather wood, water, and food.

Girls continued to help their mothers throughout their entire lives. Apache parents rarely punished their children. But they expected their children to be obedient, respectful, and helpful.

Apache babies on cradleboards

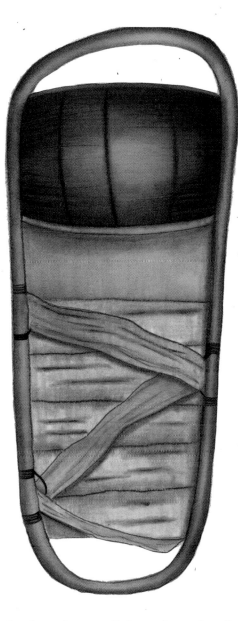

An Apache cradleboard made of wood and leather strips

Myths

The Apache never spoke the name of a dead relative. They believed that looking at dead people or touching their possessions could bring sickness. The dead were "put away" as quickly as possible in **arroyos** or cracks in rocks.

Like most Native Americans, the Apache considered owls bad luck and messengers of bad news. They did not tell jokes or stories about owls. It was bad luck to even talk about them. They believed that the ghosts of dead people lived in owls.

The dead spoke to the living through the owl's hoots and cries. Those who heard the cries could become sick and die. Only a special **medicine man** who got his powers from owls could cure them.

To the Apache, owls were mysterious creatures

War

The Apache were warriors. When they first moved to the desert, the Zuni called them "apaches du nabahu" or "**raiders** of the field."

Apache raiding parties were usually 4 to 12 men. They could travel up to 70 miles (113 km) a day. Apache raiders were experts at hiding, tracking, and leaving no sign of their passing.

On a raid, the Apache slipped silently into an enemy camp and took what they pleased. They especially liked to take horses. If an Apache raider was killed, his mother's family had the duty to take **revenge**.

Because their raiding parties were so small, the Apache avoided big battles. Instead, they fought a hit-and-run style of warfare. If the enemy was strong and ready for an attack, the Apache would wait for another chance. The Apache only fought if they had the advantage.

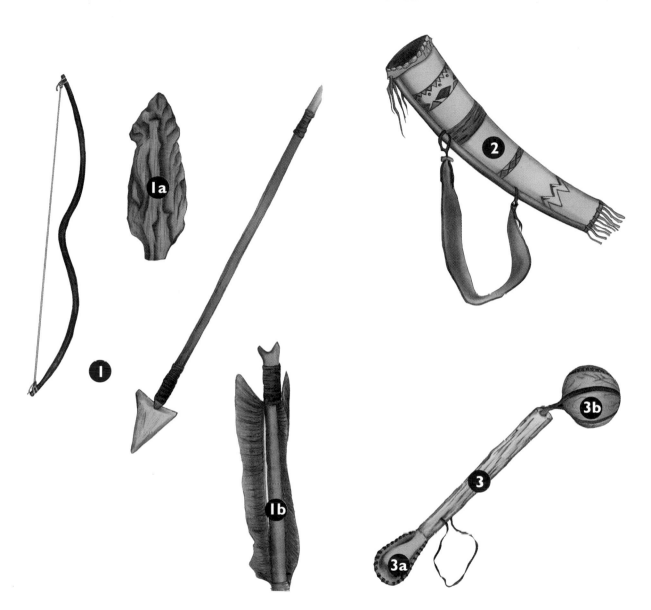

Apache weapons: 1. Bow and arrow with (1a.) flint arrowhead and (1b.) fletching made of feathers. The arrowheads and feathers were bound to the wooden arrow shaft with strips of animal hide. 2. Leather arrow quiver 3. War club with (3a.) leather handle and (3b.) leather-wrapped clubhead of stone or wood

23

Contact with Europeans

In the 1600s, the Spanish built villages and **missions** on Apache lands. Their invasion led to Apache **raids** and war.

The Spanish sent Apache **captives** deep into southern Mexico as slaves. A deep hatred developed between the Apache and Spanish. This hatred continued after Mexico became an independent country in 1821.

After the war with Mexico in 1848, America took control of the Apache lands. In 1861, near Apache Pass in New Mexico, a raiding party drove off cattle belonging to a white rancher. It also kidnapped a **ranch hand's** child. Cochise, an Apache, was wrongfully accused of the act.

Lieutenant George Bascom of the U.S. Army ordered Cochise and five of his relatives to appear for questioning. Cochise did as the lieutenant ordered. He wanted to clear his name. But, Bascom arrested the Apaches.

Cochise escaped. But, his relatives were hung. Cochise saw the hanging from a distant ridge. This hanging started a 25-year war. Thousands of Apaches and hundreds of American and Mexican settlers died.

Cochise did not **surrender** until the Chiricahua **Reservation** was formed in 1872. He died there June 8, 1874. Then, the rest of the Apache people were sent to different reservations.

A portrait of Cochise

Geronimo

There were many powerful Apache leaders. Besides Cochise, there were the warriors Juh, Del Che (Red Ant), Victorio, and the female warrior Lozen. But, Geronimo was the most famous Apache leader.

Geronimo was the last of the great Apache war chiefs. He was born in 1823 near the Gila River in present-day Arizona. His Apache name was Goyathlay, which means "one who yawns."

Geronimo was born into the Bedonkohe **band** of the Chiricahua Apache. The Mexicans gave him the name Geronimo. They feared him because of his courage and daring in battle.

In 1858, Geronimo joined the Chiricahua chief Cochise. Soon, Geronimo became an important leader during the war with the United States. When Cochise died in 1874, Geronimo refused to **surrender** and live on a **reservation**. He continued to fight against the U.S. Army until August 1886.

Geronimo and the surviving members of his band were sent to **reservations**. First, they went to one in Florida. Then, they were sent to reservations in Alabama and Oklahoma. In Oklahoma, members were held as prisoners of war until 1913.

As he grew old, Geronimo became famous. In 1905, he rode in a Washington, D.C., parade that celebrated the election of President Theodore Roosevelt. Geronimo died on February 17, 1909, at Fort Sill, Oklahoma. He is buried with many of his Chiricahua people.

Geronimo around 1905

The Apache Today

Today, many Apache live on and off of **reservations**. Apache reservations are found in Arizona, New Mexico, and Oklahoma. There are about 35,000 Apache people. The Apache reservations have almost 4.5 million acres (1.8 million ha).

The largest reservation is the San Carlos Reservation in Arizona. It has almost 1.8 million acres (720,000 ha) and about 8,100 people.

Fort Apache Reservation in Arizona is the second largest. It has twice as many people as San Carlos. The Apache call this reservation the White Mountain Apache Reservation. It has 1.6 million acres (640,000 ha) and about 16,700 people. The smallest reservation belongs to the Tonto Apache Tribe in Arizona. It has 140 people, and only 85 acres (34 ha).

The Tribal Chairman

An Apache elder on the
Jicarilla Apache Reservation

A "Gahan" dance,
the dance of the
mountain spirit

Many of the Apache **reservations** have museums and **cultural** centers. These places help preserve and teach the Apache culture. Some museums have **exhibits** with large pictures taken in the late 1800s. These photos make you feel like you are stepping back in time.

The exhibits show how the Apache dressed, and the homes they lived in. These exhibitions often display old bows and arrows, arrowheads, baskets, and other things that were a part of daily life.

Tourism is important to the Apache. The White Mountain Apache have a ski resort. It makes money for the community and creates jobs for its members. Visitors can tour the **reservation's cultural** centers and museums. They can visit historic sites and see old forts. Or, they can boat, hunt, and fish in recreation areas.

An Apache girl in
traditional dress

Many of the **reservations** have special public events. The Jicarilla Apache Reservation in New Mexico has an event in July called the Little Beaver Roundup. This event has a **rodeo**, arts and crafts, Apache dances, and a foot race.

The Apache people are working to **preserve** their culture. Many also become doctors, lawyers, teachers—and just about anything else people want to become.

An Apache dancer

An Apache cowboy herds cattle into a corral.

An Apache rodeo

Glossary

ally - a person, group, or nation united with another for some special purpose.
arc - any part of the curved line of a circle or of any curve.
arroyo - a water-carved ditch.
band - a number of persons acting together; a subgroup of a tribe.
bond - anything that ties, binds, or unites.
breechcloth - a strip of cloth or buckskin wrapped around the waist and held with a belt.
captive - a person or animal captured and held unwillingly.
coil - to wind around and around into a pile, a tube, or a curl.
concho - a round, flat piece of silver jewelry, often strung together and decorated with turquoise.
cradleboard - a decorated flat board with a wooden band at the top that protects the baby's head.
culture - the customs, arts, and tools of a nation or people at a certain time.
disciplined - developed and trained by instruction and excercise.
exhibit - a thing or things shown publicly.
fiber - a thread-like part.
fringe - a border or trimming made of threads or cords, either loose or tied together in small bunches.
medicine man - a spiritual leader of a tribe or nation.
mission - a center or headquarters for religious work.
orphan - a child whose parents are dead.
petticoat - a skirt worn beneath a dress.
poncho - a large piece of cloth or other material with a slit in the middle for the head to go through.
preserve - to keep from harm or change.
raid - a sudden attack.
ranch hand - a person hired to work on a ranch.
reservation - land set aside by the U.S. government to be lived on only by a Native American tribe.
resource - the natural material wealth of a country.
retaliate - to pay back a wrong or injury.
revenge - harm done in return for a wrong.
rodeo - a contest or exhibition of skill in roping cattle or riding horses and bulls.
sapling - a young tree or bush, that is strong but flexible.
serape - an outer garment like a cloak or poncho, often brightly colored and worn by men.
surrender - to give up.
tan - to make a hide into leather by soaking it in a special liquid.
tourism - the business of providing services for people who travel.
tradition - the handing down of beliefs, customs, and stories from parents to children.
varnish - a liquid that gives a smooth, glossy appearance to wood.

Web Sites

The official Web site of the Yavapai-Apache Nation: **http://www.yavapai-apache-nation.com/**

The Wild Apache Web site is a good source for information on the Apache and other Native American peoples: **http://www.wildapache.net/**

These sites are subject to change. Go to your favorite search engine and type in "Apache" for more sites.

Index

A

Aravaipa Apache 4
Army, U.S. 24, 26

B

Bascom, George 24

C

children 16, 18
Chiricahua Apache 4, 26, 27
Chiricahua Reservation 25
clans 4, 6
clothing 12, 29
Cochise 24, 25, 26
Coyotero Apache 4
cradleboard 18
crafts 14, 16, 24, 30

D

Dilzhee (Tonto) Apache 4

E

Europeans 12, 16, 24

F

family 6, 8, 14, 16, 18, 22
food 10, 16

Fort Apache Reservation 28

G

gardens 10
Geronimo 26, 27
guns 12

H

homes 8, 29
hunting 10

J

Jicarilla Apache 4
Jicarilla Apache Reservation 30

L

Lipan Apache 4
Little Beaver Roundup 30

M

marriage 16
medicine man 20
Mescalero Apache 4
Mexicans 25, 26
Mimbreños Apache 4
museums 29
myths 20

R

raids 22
reservations 25, 26, 27, 28, 29, 30
rodeo 30
Roosevelt, Theodore 27

S

San Carlos Reservation 28
Spanish 10, 24
Sunrise Ceremony 6

T

Tonto Apache Reservation 28
trading 12
traditions 6
tulapai 10

W

war 22, 24, 25, 26
White Mountain Apache Reservation 28, 29
wickiup 8